In our C...
(A Little B...

Compiled by Sally Featherstone
In partnership with alc associates

Illustrations by Martha Hardy

In Our Community
ISBN 1905 019 39 4

©Featherstone Education Ltd, 2006
Text ©Sally Featherstone, 2002/2006
Series Editor, Sally Featherstone
'Little Books at Home' is a trade mark of Featherstone Education Ltd.

First published in the UK, July 2006

All rights reserved. No part of this publication may be reproduced, by any means, stored in a retrieval system, or transmitted in any form or by any means, electronic, mechanical, photocopying, recording or otherwise, without the prior written consent of the copyright holder.

Published in the United Kingdom by
Featherstone Education Ltd.
44 - 46 High Street
Husbands Bosworth
Leicestershire
LE17 6LP

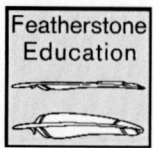

Contents

Activity **page**

Introduction 4 & 5

Bonfire Night in the Park - *an autumn celebration* 6 & 7

On a Sunny Day - *shadow play outside* 8 & 9

Rhymes and Games - *keep traditional songs alive* 10 & 11

Growing up - *starting with history* 12 & 13

In Our Street - *take a stroll* 14 & 15

Make Bird feeders - *a winter gift for birds* 16 & 17

Let's do it Outside! - *art activities in the garden* 18 & 19

Here's the Weather Forecast - *weather watch at home* 20 & 21

Pancake Race - *make and eat pancakes together* 22 & 23

Carnival! - *fun on parade* 24 & 25

Hide and Find - *an egg hunt* 26 & 27

Technology Spotters - *how does technology help us?* 28 & 29

Let's Make a Picnic - *sandwiches for everyone* 30 & 31

With Love from Me to You - *writing letters and cards* 32 & 33

Sing, Sing, What Shall we Sing? - *music at home* 34 & 35

Who Comes Down our Street? - *living and working* 36 & 37

Little Books at Home: In Our Community - Featherstone Education

Introduction

The most important gift you can give your child is your time. Research into how children learn tells us that talking, doing things and playing with their parents gives them the best start to learning, and the best preparation for school. Children whose parents are interested in them and spend time with them do better at school, and just a little time each week will make a real difference.

The activities that parents and children do together should be fun. You may think that you need special training or equipment to help your child - you do not! Simple activities, using everyday things can be the best, and they are certainly the most enjoyable. Think of the things you enjoyed doing as a child, playing in the garden, park, seaside or woods; using the things in the kitchen cupboard, making up games, songs and rhymes. These are still among the top favourites for young children today.

Some activities that help early learning are:
- ☺ playing, making up games and having fun
- ☺ saying and using new words
- ☺ singing simple songs and saying rhymes
- ☺ trying things out and talking about what happens
- ☺ looking closely at objects and living things
- ☺ exploring and experimenting together
- ☺ talking about the things you see and do together

- ☺ looking at books and telling stories
- ☺ drawing, writing, painting and making things
- ☺ playing with dough, clay, water, bubbles, chalk
- ☺ simple cooking and making things to eat

So when you have some time to spend with your child (or children), Little Books at Home give you a range of simple, enjoyable activities for young children to do with you at home.

In Our Community offers a selection of well tried ideas for exploring your community. The activities are best done where and when you have some time to explore, walk and talk without pressure. Almost all the ideas take place outside. Each page tells you what your child will be practising and learning about.

In these activities you can concentrate on playing, investigating, exploring and talking about what happens in your community - what it is like, who lives there and what goes on. There are also ideas for celebrations, parties and other activities to enjoy with your neighbours and friends.

You do not need special equipment for the activities, just the things you will find locally or in your home. If you haven't got something in the equipment list, use something else, or choose a different activity - they are all fun to do and your child will learn things from each of them.

Bonfire Night in the Park

There are lots of festivals in the autumn, and some have the additional excitement of fireworks. Use a special occasion to talk about light and fire safety.

Safety advice

! Go to an organised firework display if you can. They are much safer, specially for young children.
! If you have a firework party at home, be very careful. Teach your children the Firework Code, and talk to them about fire safety. Always supervise burning candles and NEVER leave children alone with any sort of flame or matches.
! If you use candles, put them in a glass jar, or use plasticene, sand or earth to hold them upright. A plant pot of sand or earth will help keep them steady if they are accidentally knocked.

This activity will help your child with: language skills, safety training and scientific exploration.

What you do

1. Talk about the party or display you are going to attend.
2. Look at some candles and night lights. Talk about why we have candles - for light, for the perfume, for decoration, for celebrations such as birthdays.
3. Light some candles and watch them burn. Warn the children to keep at a safe distance and never to light candles by themselves.
4. When you go outside for the fireworks, talk about what you can see - traffic and car lights, street lights, lighted windows, stars and perhaps the moon.
5. During the firework display, watch the shapes and patterns of the fireworks so you can talk about them later.
6. When you get back home, use some of the words from the **'Chatter Box'** to help your children think and talk about what happened and what they saw.

Some more ideas:
* Make some firework pictures with glitter and glue.

'Chatter Box'

* light
* rocket
* pet
* indoors
* bonfire
* party
* flames
* danger
* dark
* sparks
* stars
* sparkle
* colours
* sky
* shoot
* bang
* gold
* pink
* blue
* purple
* silver
* hand
* home
* late

The Firework Code

1. Plan your firework display to make it safe and enjoyable.
2. Keep fireworks in a closed box and use them one at a time.
3. Read and follow the instructions on each firework using a torch if necessary.
4. Light the firework at arm's length with a taper and stand well back.
5. Keep naked flames, including cigarettes, away from fireworks.
6. Never return to a firework once it has been lit.
7. Don't put fireworks in pockets and never throw them.
8. Direct rocket fireworks well away from spectators.
9. Never use paraffin or petrol on a bonfire.
10. Make sure that the fire is out and surroundings are made safe before leaving.

Little Books at Home: In Our Community - Featherstone Education

On a Sunny Day

Choose a sunny day in Autumn, Winter, Spring or Summer, to explore shadows outside with your child. If it's very hot, remember sun screen and hats to protect you all.

What you need

* a sunny day
Remember that the best fun is in making shadows with your own bodies, hands, feet, fingers. Add some dressing up clothes - hats, crowns, glasses, capes, coats etc so you can make your shadows look really different.

* you could also look at the shadows of garden furniture, toys, anything that makes a shadow

This activity will help your child with: language skills, imagination, observation and scientific exploration.

What you do

1. Find a flat place in the sun where you can see the shadows well. It could be a path, patio or even a wall.
2. Help your child to make shadows and look at how they can make their shadow move. Try jumping, crouching down, standing up tall.
3. Now try these challenges:
   jump on each others' shadows;
   hold hands without touching;
   put your hand on someone else's shadow;
   make your shadow as big and as small as you can.
4. Walk round your yard or garden, or visit the park and look for more shadows. Look at leaves, trees, flowers, bushes and other natural objects. Look at a bicycle, a stroller, swings, slides. Try making your shadow go down the slide shadow or hide it behind a tree.
5. Make your hands and fingers into shadow animals on walls and fences.

'Chatter Box'

* shadow
* tallest
* shape
* shortest
* same
* different
* outline
* biggest
* still
* smallest
* move
* long
* steps
* pattern
* shade
* shine
* moves
* round
* time

Some more ideas

* Use some thick chalk to draw round each other's shadows.
* Make a sundial by pushing a stick in a plant pot of soil and marking where the shadow moves each hour.
* Make some shadow puppets from cereal boxes by cutting out shapes and figures and holding them in front of a strong lamp to make shadows on the wall.

Little Books at Home: In Our Community - Featherstone Education

Rhymes and Games

Playing singing and action games with your children will help them at school. It will also keep traditional rhymes and songs alive, so think back to the ones you played!

What you need

* no equipment, just some memories and a sense of fun

Here are some ideas:
* 'The Grand Old Duke of York'
* 'Ring-a-Roses'
* 'Oranges and Lemons'
* 'The Big Ship Sails through the Alley O'
* 'Do you Know the Muffin Man?'
* 'In and Out the Dusty Bluebells'

This activity will help your child with: language skills, memory, taking turns and listening. They will also learn a sense of history from finding out what you did in the past.

What you do

1. All these songs and games are rooted in the past and will give a starting point to talk about events that happened long ago.
2. You may find that friends, neighbours and family members know other circle games which are local to your area or which are played in other parts of the world. Invite them to join in and teach you the words and actions!
3. Try some other games from the past such as hopscotch, marbles, jacks (sometimes called Snobs, Fivestones or Dabstones), spinning tops, skipping games, even conkers!
4. Visit your library and ask if they have a nursery rhyme or song book. They may have a tape or CD to borrow as well. Then you could take a portable CD player out in the garden or park and have a really good time!
5. Get the children to ring grandparents, aunts and uncles and ask them if they know any rhymes and songs.
6. Sing pop songs and signature tunes from your favourite TV programmes. Make up your own words and movements or just clap and 'La-la-la' to the tune.

'Chatter Box'

* game
* rhyme
* song
* past
* time
* long ago
* history
* turn
* line
* circle
* ring
* clap
* castle
* turns
* dance
* sing
* action
* favourite
* next
* partner

Some more ideas

* Try the singing game 'There was a Princess Long Ago' or the nursery rhyme 'London Bridge is Falling Down' as you build a castle in the sand pit.
* Sing action songs such as 'Wind the Bobbin' and 'Oats and Beans' which are related to work in the past.
* Borrow The Little Book of Nursery Rhymes from your child's nursery or school.

Growing Up

Children are fascinated by photos and stories of the time before they were born. Share some memories with them and talk about what you were like when you were a child.

What you need

* pictures and photos of your family - babies, children, grandparents, parents.
* photos of you as a baby or as a child.
* if you haven't got any photos of yourself, use magazine photos of babies to talk about when you were a child.

This activity will help your child with: language skills, a sense of time and a sense of their own identity and family.

What you do

1. Sit together somewhere comfortable to talk about the photos you have collected. These could be a family album or just a collection of single photos.
2. Take your time as you look at the photos, say the names of the people and explain how they are related to you. Young children find it difficult to think of you as a child or of you having a mum and dad!
3. Talk about what you did when you were a child - where you lived, your friends, the games you played. Children love to hear stories of your childhood, specially if you ever got into trouble!
4. Play a game of 'Guess who?'. Show a picture and see if they can tell you who it is. Start with more recent photos before you show baby photos of people who are adults now!
5. Talk about the features of the people in the photos - their hair, eye colour, clothing, height etc.
6. Show your children pictures of themselves when they were younger, and tell them stories about what they did, what they ate, what they liked, their favourite toys.

'Chatter Box'

* baby
* toddler
* child
* teenager
* adult
* grown up
* younger
* older
* same
* different
* guess
* grandma
* grandad
* mum
* dad
* brother
* sister
* cousin
* auntie
* uncle
* before
* after
* looks like
* family

Some more ideas

* Make a family tree poster on your fridge door, with photos of all your family members in the right order, so your children can see who they are and get a real sense of family.
* Write family birthdays on a wall calendar so your children can begin to take a part in remembering special days. Add other significant days such as anniversaries, holidays etc.

Little Books at Home: In Our Community - Featherstone Education

In Our Street

Go for a gentle walk around your neighbourhood with your child, and see how many different sorts of signs, notices and other sorts of writing you can find.

What you need

* no special resources - you could take a camera to record what you see, but this isn't essential
* some uninterrupted time

This activity will help your child with: reading and writing, a sense of direction and a sense of community.

What you do

1. Take your children on a walk in your neighbourhood. Ask them to look out for notices signs and other writing.
2. Take time during the walk to talk about the signs and what they mean.
3. Look at the different sorts of street furniture (bins, post boxes, seats, fire hydrants, manhole covers etc) and what they are for. Are they to help people to:
   - ? find their way around,
   - ? move and play safely
   - ? know where things are kept
   - ? look after the environment
   - ? rest and relax

   or are they for services such as electricity, water or fire?
4. If you have a camera, you could take some photographs of all the things you see.
5. Make some signs from paper and cocktail sticks or twigs, so you can use them with cars and other toys to make roads and streets.

'Chatter Box'

* street
* sign
* writing
* notice
* letters
* read
* name
* road
* lane
* house
* shop
* direction
* traffic light
* zebra crossing
* post box
* light
* stop
* go

Some more ideas

* Make a map together of your local streets and houses. Use some wallpaper or lining paper.
* Make some signs for the doors in your house - eg 'This is Nathan's Room', 'Please keep the bathroom tidy', 'Please shut this door'.
* Encourage everyone in the house to write signs and notices - why not make a menu for Sunday dinner?

Little Books at Home: In Our Community - Featherstone Education

Make Bird Feeders

Attracting birds to your garden is a very rewarding thing to do. You will save the lives of birds during the winter, and it's fun too!

What you need

* bird food – seeds, nuts, breadcrumbs
* bird feeders – made or bought
* binoculars
* illustrated books about birds
* clip and white boards

This activity will help your child with: observation and scientific exploration. They will also need to develop a sense of responsibility, so they don't forget to put food out regularly.

What you do

1. Talk with your children about what they already know about birds.
2. Look at pictures of common garden birds and help the children to notice how they differ from one another. Talk about colour - the size, shape or colour of their beaks, legs, feathers etc.
3. Talk about what birds like to eat, and where they might find their food. Go shopping for some bird food.
4. Look at the bird food you have bought – talk about the size, shape, colour and texture of the nuts and seeds.
5. Go out into the garden or back yard and decide together where to put your bird feeders. You will want to be able to see them easily from indoors, but they need to be high enough up to be safe from cats.
6. Stand quietly by the window and wait to see if birds come. Breakfast time is a good time to see which birds come.

'Chatter Box'

* bird
* beak
* wing
* head
* feet
* food
* breast
* feather
* tail
* seed
* nut
* peanut
* water
* hang
* table
* hook
* window
* peck
* nest
* baby
* hatch

Some more ideas

* Borrow or buy some inexpensive binoculars, so you can see the birds better.
* Go to the library and get a bird book to help with your spotting.
* Make some Bird Cake by mixing bird seed and breadcrumbs with melted fat. Press into yogurt pots or plastic cups and cool before hanging them up with string.

Little Books at Home: In Our Community - Featherstone Education

Let's do it Outside!

Art activities are much more fun if you do them outside - and if you go out into your community, you may make some friends who like doing the same things as you do.

What you need

* chalk for pavement pictures
* and for hangings, weavings and natural constructions, look for string, twigs, feathers, grass, leaves, small stones, broken crockery, bark, moss etc

Remember - only use natural materials that are NOT still growing! Remind your children not to pick growing plants or flowers.

This activity will help your child with: creativity and making friends. They will also learn to notice more of the world around them and how much fun they can have with free natural materials.

What you do

1. You could make a chalk picture on your front path or even on the pavement (as long as you don't upset your neighbours!).
2. When you go out for a walk, always take a plastic bag in your pocket and collect sticks, leaves, grasses, cones etc as you go.
3. At some point during your walk (beside a park bench, on a woodland path, by a gate) stop and make a picture with the things you have collected. You could:
    hang leaves and grasses from a tree
    thread sticks and feathers through a fence
    make a pattern on the ground with leaves and stones
    make a path of fallen leaves all the way home
4. Take a piece of string each and thread or tie leaves and twigs to it to remind you of your walk.
5. Take a reel of cotton with you; wind it round stones, twigs and leaves and hang them in trees and bushes.

'Chatter Box'

* collect
* pattern
* hang
* leaf
* cone
* same
* different
* square
* circle
* spiral
* string
* thread

* bag
* pocket
* pebble
* stone
* colour
* shape
* remember

Some more ideas

* Use sticks to make patterns and pictures in beach sand or mud.
* Collect shells and stones for a beach picture - make it big enough and other families may come and help you!
* Use decorators' brushes, small sprays and a bucket of water to paint water pictures on walls, paths and fences. These will disappear quickly leaving no trace!

Here's the Weather Forecast

You could either watch the weather for a day or make a longer term commitment to this fascinating aspect, which affects all our lives.

What you need for a weather station

* card, scissors, pen
* a garden cane
* an empty plastic bottle
* a broom handle
* a bucket of sand or earth
* some chalk
* ribbons or strips of fabric (from an old shirt or other old clothing)

This activity will help your child with: language skills, imagination, observation and scientific exploration. They will also need to learn how to predict and check if they were right!

What you do

1. Talk about the weather every day with your family.
2. As you go to school or nursery, look for signs of the weather.
3. Watch the weather forecast on TV or listen to the radio and see what they think the weather will be like.
4. Look for photos of the weather in newspapers, books and magazines
5. Look at the clouds and other signs of what is happening outside, before you go out.
6. Make your own weather station for your garden, terrace, balcony or yard:
    * make a sundial by standing a broom handle in a bucket of sand or earth
    * hang up strips of cloth or ribbons to see how hard the wind is blowing
    * make a windmill and hang some ribbons up for the wind.
    * cut the top off a plastic bottle, turn it upside down and put it back in the bottle bottom to make a rain gauge
    * make a simple windmill from card.

'Chatter Box'

* weather
* rainy
* windy
* sunny
* snowy
* foggy
* cloudy
* misty
* shadow
* rain gauge
* windmill
* puddle
* raindrop
* rainbow
* ice
* snow
* frost
* wind
* sun
* cloud
* thunder
* lightning
* flood
* hail

Some more ideas

* Watch the TV forecast each day and see if they were right! Give them a point each time they are.
* Make a weather chart for a week, stick it on the fridge door and fill it in each day (you may have to divide the day into more than one bit as our weather is so changeable!).
* Get some travel brochures and talk about the weather in other countries.

Little Books at Home: In Our Community - Featherstone Education

Pancake Race

You don't need to save a Pancake Race till Pancake Day! Most children (and their families) love pancakes and will eat them any time. Vary the fillings to suit tastes.

What you need

* a sunny day
* a fork or whisk, a bowl, a frying pan
* a fish slice, a big spoon
* lemon juice and sugar, or jam, banana slices, honey, grated cheese for fillings
* The Enormous Pancake story

Ingredients for 16 pancakes:
225g/8oz plain flour (sifted)
2 eggs
a pint of milk
a pinch of salt
a drop of sunflower oil or a knob of melted butter

This activity will help your child with: language skills, planning, observation, cooking skills and scientific exploration.

What you do

Pancake Day/Shrove Tuesday (also called Mardi Gras) is celebrated on the last day before Lent begins on Ash Wednesday. Lent is a time when Christian people think about Jesus and eat very simple food. On Pancake Tuesday people eat up all the rich foods left before Lent.

1. Wash your hands.
2. Measure the flour together, put it in the bowl and make a dip in the middle with a spoon.
3. Break the egg into the dip in the flour, and add the milk. Gradually mix the flour into the milk and egg with the spoon, then use a fork or whisk to whisk the mixture - it should be quite runny, and may need a bit more milk or water.
4. Heat the oil in the frying pan (adult only) and drop a spoonful of mixture in. You can do several smaller pancakes each time (if they just can't wait!) or one big one.
5. Turn the pancakes with the fish slice after about 3 mins to cook the other side - or you could toss them to turn them over (easier with only one pancake!).
6. Add fillings of your choice and eat.
7. If you want to have a race, use cold pans and cold pancakes.

'Chatter Box'

- Shrove Tuesday
- Lent
- pancake
- celebrate
- mix
- batter
- toss/turn
- filling
- favourite
- careful
- delicious
- count
- cook
- measure
- taste
- smell
- lemon
- balance
- winner
- race
- drop

Some more ideas

- Have a pancake party and invite your neighbours.
- Read or tell the story of The Enormous Pancake.
- Experiment with fillings - sweet and savoury.
- Pancakes make great picnic food. Cook them in advance, wrap them in a cloth and add fillings when you get to the picnic, or fill and roll them and put them in a plastic box.

Little Books at Home: In Our Community - Featherstone Education

Carnival!

This is a excuse to have fun in your garden, park or neighbourhood. Contact neighbours, friends or local groups to arrange a carnival or just have one in the garden for fun!

What you need

* a sunny day
* costumes; these could be:
  - scarves, shoes and other clothes
  - dressing up clothes
  - simple costumes made from paper or fabric
* paper plates for masks
* hats
* some recorded music or home made instruments

This activity will help your child with: language skills, imagination, and understanding about celebration. It's also great fun, and fun helps learning!

What you do

1. Explain to the children that carnivals are happy times, where everyone comes together and has a big party, often in the streets. Ask the children if they can remember parties you have been to and how parties make you feel.
2. Show them how they can make a carnival mask to wear at the parade. Pre-cut eyeholes in different shaped strips of paper or paper plates, and let the children decorate them with pens, crayons or paint.
3. You could help the children to create their own costumes to go with their masks. Use bits of fabric, scarves, pyjamas, hats etc. Talk about how they can make their costume more interesting by sticking things on or adding jewellery.
4. Explain that at the carnivals they sometimes have floats to carry people through the street parties. Put some chairs in a line, decorate them with strips of brightly coloured crepe paper and fabrics. Sit on the float in your costumes and wave to the crowds!

'Chatter Box'

* carnival
* parade
* music
* masks
* costumes
* floats
* band
* instruments
* decorate
* noisy
* sing
* dance
* watch
* play
* march
* line
* fancy
* hats

Some more ideas

* Make some carnival music to dance to. Use some home made instruments (saucepans, wooden spoons, tins, metal trays), or try clapping, slapping knees, clicking to get into the carnival mood!
* Use large boxes to make a moving float for your parade.
* Make flags from old clothing or sheets and paint them with patterns so you can wave them at the carnival street parade.

Hide and Find

Have fun in your garden or the park with a simple egg hunt. You could do it at Easter or in Spring, but children enjoy this sort of activity at any time of year - even in the snow!

What you need

* foil covered mini-eggs, wooden or plastic eggs or real hard-boiled eggs
* paper or card and pens for the clues
* a basket for each child to collect the eggs they find
* you could also make a rabbit footprint template

This activity will help your child with: language skills, maths language and perseverance.

What you do

Your preparation:
* Find some pictures or examples of decorated eggs to talk about. Look for books and stories about Spring and eggs.
* Now set up the egg hunt. Write a clue for each of the places where you are going to hide the eggs. Put the first one in an envelope, then hide the others - put the clue for the next egg with each of the eggs to help the children to find them. The clues could be pictures or words - such as 'under the big bush', 'by the shed', or 'on the step'.

1. Now talk to your children about the Easter Bunny, and tell them sometimes eggs are found in children's gardens.
2. Show the children the envelope and say they have had some post today. Read the children the first clue that will help them find the first egg and the next clue.
3. Help the children to work out the clues and find the eggs. Collect these in a basket (Remind the children not to eat the eggs as they find them!) - this may be difficult!
4. Make sure that there are enough eggs for each child and each adult in the family.
5. When the children have found all the eggs, bring the basket back inside and share the eggs!

'Chatter Box'

* Easter
* chocolate
* eggs
* hide/find
* share
* clues
* collect
* Spring
* Bunny
* footprint
* count
* more
* basket
* prize
* puzzle
* look
* under
* behind
* covered
* carefully

Some more ideas

* Hard boil some eggs and let the children decorate them with food colouring or felt pens.
* Have an Easter egg race, rolling your eggs down a slope to see which one gets to the bottom first.
* Break open a raw egg with the children to see what it looks like inside. Talk about the creatures that grow lay eggs and the names of the babies.

Little Books at Home: In Our Community - Featherstone Education

Technology Spotters

Help your children to recognise all the ways that technology helps us in our communities. Take a walk and see how many you can spot near your home.

What you need

* just a notebook and pen, or a camera

This activity will help your child with: language skills, ICT, observation and exploration.

What you do

Technology is everywhere. Children are excited about technology, but they also take it for granted. What we think is amazing, children treat as normal. We remember a time when some things weren't possible, because the technology had not been invented - being able to phone someone from anywhere on a mobile phone, using a microwave, taking a digital photo.

1. Start in your own home:
   - Your own home will have masses of technology. Look at microwaves, telephones, word processors, security alarms and cameras, door locks, photocopiers, fax machines, CD players, videos, phones etc. Point out the ways we use technology to help us.
2. Walk down your street and around your community:
   - Look at crossing signs, traffic lights, security cameras, parking barriers, meters, petrol pumps, street signs, electronic doors on shops etc. Talk about what they do, and what it would be like without them.
3. Take a special look:
   - When you visit the supermarket, petrol station, cinema, electrical store, DIY store, look at tills, automatic and revolving doors, pagers, intercoms, phones, scanners, scales, ticket printers, security cameras, lifts, signs, escalators etc. Talk about what they are for and how they work.

'Chatter Box'

* look
* different
* same
* switch
* camera
* display
* telephone
* electricity
* phone
* on/off
* light
* heat
* power
* wire
* cable
* move
* help
* sign
* easy
* timer

Some more ideas

* Take photographs while you are with the children of the different technologies, and use the photographs to make a book or stick them on a door so you can remember them.
* Keep spotting technology as you travel, shop, visit or walk around. help your children to be aware of the wonderful things technology can help us to do.

Little Books at Home: In Our Community - Featherstone Education

Let's Make a Picnic

The choice of fillings for sandwiches is endless, and sandwiches are very easy for children to make. Look in your supermarket for different kinds of bread to extend the choices.

What you need

* ready sliced bread
* soft margarine or butter
* chopping board or clean work surface
* dessert knives for spreading
* bowls and spoons for fillings
* fillings to choose: younger children could start with easy ones such as sliced cucumber, Marmite, cheese spread or jam. Older children will be able to manage chopped hard boiled egg, grated cheese etc

This activity will help your child with: sequencing, hand control and independence.

What you do

1. Look at the bread together and share new words to describe how it smells, feels, looks. Use words like crust, crumbs, slice.
2. Give each child two slices of bread.
3. If they need it, show them how to use the knife to spread the butter/margarine over both slices of bread.
4. Encourage them to work carefully to cover the whole area. Some children become VERY absorbed in this - give them time, this may be their first sandwich!
5. If they need it, help them to cover one slice with the filling, place the second slice on top and <u>gently</u> press down.
6. Most children will be able to cut their sandwich by themselves. Talk about the shapes they can make by cutting them in different ways. Use half, quarter, square, triangle.
7. Arrange the sandwich on a plate before eating, or take your sandwiches outside for a picnic in the garden or park. Children love making their own sandwiches and will often eat more if they have prepared it themselves.

'Chatter Box'

* bread
* butter
* filling
* like
* different
* choose
* make
* by myself
* by yourself
* knife
* careful
* cut
* picnic
* drink
* blanket
* park
* garden
* shape
* half
* quarter

Some more ideas

* Use cutters to cut sandwiches into animal or other shapes. You could also try cutting a shape in the top slice to reveal the filling!
* Make sandwiches for a party or special event.
* Try a variety of different breads: wholemeal, sliced and unsliced, granary, rye, seeded.
* Toasted sandwiches are good for a quick winter picnic in the garden.

Little Books at Home: In Our Community - Featherstone Education

With Love from Me to You

Making and sending letters and cards is good fun, involves a lot of skills and helps children to see that learning to read and write are important skills to practice.

What you need

* a collection of things that have come through your letter box - junk mail, bills, letters, cards, invitations, reminders
* paper, card, old or new envelopes, pens, pencils, crayons, scissors, glue stick

This activity will help your child with: language skills, writing, social skills.

What you do

1. Talk about the things that come through your letter box, and read some of them with your child.
2. Sit with them while you write a note or letter to send to someone you know. Let them add their name, a picture or a card of their own.
3. Leave the materials so they can make their own letters and cards. These could be for family, friends, teachers, neighbours, grandparents - anyone they know.
4. Help them with words of they ask you, but encourage them to do as much as they can on their own.
5. Deliver the letters and cards together - so children are safe - send them by post, deliver them in person, put them through letterboxes. You could even scan them and send them by e-mail.
6. Everyone loves getting letters and cards from children, so help them to make it a habit, then they may get letters back, that's a real treat for them!

'Chatter Box'

* letter
* card
* from
* to
* read
* write
* picture
* send
* letter box
* postman
* stamp
* deliver
* pleased
* thank you
* invitation
* postcard
* stick
* envelope
* reply
* list

Some more ideas

* Encourage your child or children to write thank you letters for gifts, holiday postcards to their teachers, invitations, lists and reminders for themselves or you. They will love it!
* Make sure your children have plenty of paper and pens so they can write things whenever they want to. Keep the equipment tidy in a plastic box with a handle.

Little Books at Home: In Our Community - Featherstone Education

Sing, Sing, What Shall we Sing?

Use simple sound makers from your home to make a band to accompany songs you sing together. You can use them indoors or outside, and even use them in a parade.

What you need

* things from your home that make good sounds:
  - pans, pan lids and tins
  - trays and boxes
  - wooden spoons
  - cartons of cereal or rice
  - plastic bowls and buckets
  - card tubes
  - old cutlery
  - bottles or plastic boxes filled with stones or dried beans

This activity will help your child with: language skills, imagination, musical skills, keeping a beat.

What you do

1. Let the children experiment with your home made instruments before you start to play games together. Some children will want to play for a long time on their own before they are ready to start working in a band!
2. When they are ready, start to play some simple games such as:
   - you play a simple pattern, they copy it;
   - they conduct you, you conduct them;
   - put on a good CD and play along to the songs;
   - march around as you play (this is more difficult);
   - take turns playing a pattern of beats;
   - use your feet too, to stamp as you play;
   - try playing different instruments in turn;
   - hop, skip or jump as you play;
   - try recording your music and playing it back.
3. Invite neighbours and friends to join your band and have a show, display or parade in your garden, park or street.
4. Keep inventing new instruments to play.

'Chatter Box'

* pan
* box
* fill
* rattle
* play
* music
* together
* turns
* pattern
* wait
* jump
* stamp
* copy
* record
* sound
* beat
* first
* march
* dance
* favourite

Some more ideas

* Take your children to hear bands and street music.
* Use your instruments to accompany music on TV or radio.
* When you go out for a walk, explore the sounds you can make - a stick on railings, two branches tapped together, shuffling through leaves, stamping on a path, clapping or humming as you walk.

Who Comes Down Our Street?

Talk with your children about the people who live and work in your street or community. Watch them come and go, and find out what they do.

What you need
* no equipment, just your eyes, ears and voices

This activity will help your child with: language skills, imagination, observation and exploration.

What you do

1. Watch from windows and front gardens as people arrive, visit and work near your home.
2. Start with regular visitors like the postman, milkman, free newspaper delivery, window cleaner. Talk about what they do and how they help us. Think about their jobs, their homes and their families. Discuss whether you think they have any children, where they might live, what they do when they are not working.
3. Talk about the job they do - where they keep their equipment, what they need to do when they have finished their work and before they can go home. Do some of them work at night or very early in the morning. Who fills the milk bottles with milk? Where does the postman get the letters from?
4. Watch the people who park near or walk past your home - Who are they? Where are they going? Who are they visiting? What are their jobs?

'Chatter Box'

* postman
* dustman
* milkman
* health visitor
* shopping
* neighbour
* next door
* delivery
* flowers
* removal
* bottles
* letters
* dustbin
* newspaper
* parking
* van
* lorry
* car
* case
* bag

Some more ideas

* Ask your regular postman or milkman about what they do, if they have a family etc.
* Spot the same cars or vans visiting - use colours (or number plates for older children) to check the regular visitors.
* Visit the library and find some picture books about people who help us - the postman, the milkman, the health visitor etc.

In Our Community

In Our Community is one of a series of Little Books at Home. The series has been developed in partnership with alc associates, who have been closely involved from the original concept.

alc associates work to promote an understanding of how children think and learn. To find out more about their work, contact them at:
   alc associates Ltd., PO Box 51, Truro, TR1 1WJ
   info@allowercase.fsbusiness.co.uk
   01872 273492 or 01872 264603